Hidden Pictures
Grades 4-6

by
Linda Standke

Carson-Dellosa Publishing, LLC

Directions

There are treasures of unspeakable value hidden in God's Word! Begin a treasure hunt by looking up the scripture reference to answer the question about each story.

Then, find and circle the story-related items hidden in the picture.

For even more treasures, read the entire story in the Bible and determine how the hidden items relate to the story. Some items are directly related, while some are just for fun (like the sunglasses in the fiery furnace).

Mission Statement

It is the mission of Carson-Dellosa Publishing to create the highest-quality Scripture-based children's products that teach the Word of God, share His love and goodness, assist in faith development, and glorify His Son, Jesus Christ.

". . . teach me your ways so I may know you. . . ."
Exodus 33:13

Credits

Project Director: Sherrill B. Flora
Editor: Carol Layton
Inside Illustrations: Julie Anderson
Cover Design: Peggy Jackson
Cover Illustration: Dan Sharp

Contents

Printed in the USA • All rights reserved.

ISBN 978-0-88724-912-9
05-003171151

Name _____

Seven-by-Seven

Some animals were taken on the ark in groups of seven (three pairs for breeding and one to sacrifice). Read **Genesis 7:2-3** to find out which kinds of animals were taken on the ark by sevens.

ark	hammer	Noah's wife	rain hat
Bible	nail	rainbow	saw
dove	Noah	raincoat	umbrella

The Lord Speaks to Jacob in a Dream

Read **Genesis 28:14** to find out who God promised to bless through Jacob and his offspring.

angel	cane	quarter moon	star
Bible	dream cloud	rock	tree
blanket	earth	stairs	zzzz's of sleep

Joseph and His Brothers

Joseph's brothers were jealous of the beautiful coat their father gave him. Read **Genesis 37:2** to find out another reason why the brothers resented Joseph.

Bible	goat	pharaoh	throne
coat	house	sack of grain	well
coins	jail bars	silver cup	wheat

Holy Ground

When the Lord spoke to Moses from the burning bush and told him to bring His people out of Egypt, Moses asked what he should say if the Israelites ask who sent him. Read **Exodus 3:14** to find out how God answered Moses' question.

Bible	match	sandals	stick
bush	Moses	sheep	sun
cloud	rock	staff	tent

Corrected by a Donkey

Read **Numbers 22:31** to find out who opened Balaam's eyes so that he could see the angel.

angel	donkey	rock	stick
angry eyes	hurt foot	sack	sword
Bible	jug	scroll	tree

Shout!

Read **Joshua 6:10** to find out what Joshua told the people NOT to do until the day that he told them to shout.

Bible	hiking boot	sandal	stone tablets
door	horn	7	tent
helmet	map	stone	walking stick

Samson "Falls" in Love

Read **Judges 16:18** to find out what the Philistines brought to Delilah in exchange for information about Samson's strength.

barbell	brush	money bag	scissors
barber's razor	comb	pillar	shampoo
Bible	flexed biceps	pillow	sword

Answering the Call

Read **1 Samuel 3:9** to find out how the priest, Eli, instructed Samuel to answer the Lord's call.

Bible	ear	lantern	robe
blanket	Eli	pillow	Samuel
candle	house	pitcher	speech bubble

10

David Shows the World

Read **1 Samuel 17:46** to find out what David said the whole world would know after the battle that day.

Bible	Goliath	sheep	sword
cross	king	shield	throne
David	sack	slingshot	water bottle

CD-2027 Hidden Pictures: 4-6

Name _____

Elijah's Sanctuary

Read **1 Kings 17:2-4** to find out how God protected and provided for the prophet, Elijah.

Bible   blanket   candy   raven

birdhouse   bread   Elijah hiding   steak

birdseed bag   campfire   glass of ice water   wineskin

Name _____

Fire Falls on Mount Carmel

Read **1 Kings 18:27** to find out how Elijah teased the prophets of the false god, Baal, when they called on Baal to bring fire to their sacrifice and nothing happened. Read **1 Kings 18:38** to find out what happened when Elijah called on God to accept his water-soaked sacrifice.

Bible	cloud	match	sun
bucket	dead tree	praying man	sword
bull	idol	praying woman	torch

    CD-2027 *Hidden Pictures: 4-6*

A Beautiful Choice

Esther was allowed to choose any outfit in the palace to wear when King Xerxes selected the new queen. Read **Esther 2:15** to find out what she chose.

bathtub	comb	hairbrush	perfume
Bible	crown	hand-held mirror	slipper
blush compact	gown	magnifying glass	sponge

Name _____

The Not-So-Fiery Furnace

King Nebuchadnezzar asked silly questions when it came to Shadrach, Meshach, and Abednego.
Read **Daniel 3:15** and **3:24** to find out what they were.

ax	garden hose	king	praying hands
Bible	glass of ice water	marshmallow	sunglasses
fire helmet	idol	match	thermometer

CD-2027 *Hidden Pictures: 4-6*

Mary's Response

Read **Luke 1:38** to find out how the Virgin Mary responded when Gabriel told her that she would give birth to a son through the power of the Holy Spirit.

angel	chair	house	needle
baby	flower vase	Joseph	plate
Bible	goblet	Mary	thread

16

Shepherds Find Baby Jesus

Read **Luke 2:17** to find out what the shepherds did when they left Mary, Joseph, and baby Jesus.

Bible	hay	shepherd	star
donkey	manger	stable	trumpet
dove	sheep	staff	wise man

Miracle for Mom

When Jesus turned water into wine at a wedding feast, only Mary and this group of people knew about the miracle. Read **John 2:9** to find out who they were.

Bible	drumstick	Jesus	ring
bride	goblet	jug	tambourine
cake	groom	oil lamp	torch

Name _____

The Thirsty Samaritan

Read **John 4:10** to find out what kind of water Jesus offered to the Samaritan woman at the well.

Bible	cup	pitcher	town
bucket	ladle	ring	well
clouds	lantern	sun	woman

CD-2027 Hidden Pictures: 4-6

Name _____

Come, Follow Me!

Jesus invited two fishermen, Simon (Peter) and Andrew, to follow Him and fish for men.
Read **Matthew 4:20** to find out how the brothers responded to His invitation.

Bible	fish	net	starfish
boat	fish symbol	oar	tackle box
bobber (float)	fishing pole	sandals	worm

Through the Roof, out the Door!

When Jesus saw the faith of the paralyzed man and his friends, He said, "Son, your sins are forgiven." This made some teachers of the law angry. Read **Mark 2:9** to find out what Jesus said to these men.

Bible	house	roof	stretcher
blanket	Jesus	rope	sun
cross	praying hands	saw	window

Name _____

Hidden Treasure

Read **Matthew 13:44** to find out what the kingdom of heaven is like.

$100 bill	crown	money bag	ring
Bible	dirt pile	mouse	shovel
coins	jewels	necklace	treasure chest

Quiet!

The disciples thought it was okay to be afraid in a boat during a bad storm. Read **Mark 4:40** to find out what Jesus had to say to them about their fear and faith.

anchor	boat	lightning	pillow
Bible	fish	net	scared disciple
blanket	Jesus sleeping	oar	storm cloud

Name _____

Jesus Is Always More Than Enough!

Read **John 6:11** to find out how much food each person received when Jesus fed over 5,000 people with five loaves of bread and two fish. Read **John 6:12** to find out Jesus' view of stewardship.

basket of bread	boat	grass	rock
Bible	boy	oar	sun
blanket	fish	praying hands	tree

24

Name _____

The Merciful Samaritan

Jesus told the story of the good Samaritan to answer the question of an expert in Jewish law. Read **Luke 10:29** to find out what the question was.

bandage	coins	inn	ointment tube
Bible	crutch	Levite	priest
club	donkey	medicine bottle	stretcher

Name _____

Zacchaeus! Come on Down!

Read **Luke 19:4** to find out what two things Zacchaeus did so that he could see Jesus.

bag of coins   goblet   palm branch   scroll

Bible   house   person praising   table

chair   leaf   plate of food   tree

26

CD-2027 Hidden Pictures: 4-6

Name _____

Jesus Who?

At the Passover meal, Peter told Jesus that he was ready to die with Him. Jesus replied that before the rooster crowed, Peter would deny three times that he even knew Him. Read **Luke 22:62** to find out what Peter did when he realized that he had done just as Jesus had said.

basket	campfire	robe	scroll
Bible	cross	rooster	servant girl
building	jug	sandals	sunrise

The Lamb of God

Read **John 19:29** to find out what plant was used during the crucifixion to minister to Jesus. Read **Exodus 12:22** to find out how this same plant was used during the first Passover.

Bible	crown of thorns	robe	stalk and sponge
cloth	dice	soldier	torn curtain
cross	perfume	spike	woman praying

He's Not Here!

Pilate ordered guards to watch the tomb because he thought Jesus' disciples might try to steal His body. When an angel appeared like lightning, the guards were so afraid that they passed out. Read **Matthew 28:5** to find out the first four words the angel spoke to the women at Jesus' empty tomb.

angel	cross	perfume	stone bench
Bible	flower	shield	sun
cloud	Mary	stone	sword

Answer Key

Clean animals and birds were taken on the ark in groups of seven.

Page 3

God blessed all people on earth through Jacob's offspring (Jesus).

Page 4

Joseph brought his father a bad report about his brothers.

Page 5

God told Moses to tell the Israelites, " 'I AM' has sent me to you."

Page 6

The LORD opened Balaam's eyes.

WHY ARE YOU HITTING ME?

Page 7

Joshua told the people not to say a word.

Page 8

The Philistines gave Delilah money (silver) for her information.

Page 9

Eli told Samuel to say, "Speak, LORD, for your servant is listening."

Samuel!

Page 10

David said the whole world would know that there is a God in Israel.

Page 11

CD-2027 Hidden Pictures: 4-6

Answer Key

The LORD told Elijah where to hide and find water, and ordered ravens to feed him.

Page 12

1. Elijah said to shout louder—maybe their god was thinking, busy, traveling, or sleeping. 2. The fire of the LORD fell and burned everything.

Page 13

Esther chose only what the king's eunuch suggested.

Page 14

The king asked, ". . . what god will be able to rescue you from my hand?" and "Weren't there three men that we tied up and threw into the fire?"

Page 15

Mary replied, "I am the Lord's servant. May it be to me as you have said."

Page 16

The shepherds spread the word about what they had been told.

Page 17

The servants who drew the water knew where the wine came from.

Page 18

Jesus offered living water to the Samaritan woman.

Page 19

Simon (Peter) and Andrew left their nets at once and followed Jesus.

Page 20

CD-2027 Hidden Pictures: 4-6

Answer Key

Jesus asked them which was easier: to say that sins were forgiven or to command a paralyzed man to walk.

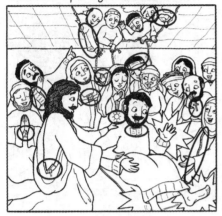

Page 21

The kingdom of heaven is like treasure hidden in a field.

Page 22

Jesus said that their fear showed that they did not have faith.

Page 23

1. The people who were seated received as much as they wanted. 2. Jesus commanded that nothing be wasted.

Page 24

The expert in Jewish law asked Jesus, "Who is my neighbor?"

Page 25

Zacchaeus ran ahead of the crowd and climbed a sycamore-fig tree.

Page 26

Peter went outside and wept bitterly.

Page 27

1. A stalk of the hyssop plant was used to give Jesus a drink. 2. Hyssop was used to put lambs' blood on the door frames.

Page 28

The angel said, "Do not be afraid."

Page 29

32

CD-2027 Hidden Pictures: 4-6